Cite
Your
Source

SUPER
QUICK
SKILLS

Cite
Your
Source

Phillip
C. Shon

Los Angeles | London | New Delhi
Singapore | Washington DC | Melbourne

Los Angeles | London | New Delhi
Singapore | Washington DC | Melbourne

SAGE Publications Ltd
1 Oliver's Yard
55 City Road
London EC1Y 1SP

SAGE Publications Inc.
2455 Teller Road
Thousand Oaks, California 91320

SAGE Publications India Pvt Ltd
B 1/I 1 Mohan Cooperative Industrial Area
Mathura Road
New Delhi 110 044

SAGE Publications Asia-Pacific Pte Ltd
3 Church Street
#10-04 Samsung Hub
Singapore 049483

Editor: Jai Seaman
Editorial assistant: Lauren Jacobs
Production editor: Tanya Szwarnowska
Marketing manager: Catherine Slinn
Design: Shaun Mercier
Typeset by: C&M Digitals (P) Ltd, Chennai, India
Printed in the UK

Library of Congress Control Number: 2018966553

British Library Cataloguing in Publication data

A catalogue record for this book is available from the
British Library

ISBN 978-1-5264-8885-5

At SAGE we take sustainability seriously. Most of our products are printed in the UK using responsibly
sourced papers and boards. When we print overseas we ensure sustainable papers are used as measured
by the PREPS grading system. We undertake an annual audit to monitor our sustainability.

Contents

Everything in this book!

Section 1   Why do I have to cite?

Will explain why you have to cite your sources— and will show you how to read adequately to give legitimacy to your arguments and claims.

Section 2   What am I supposed to cite?

You will be introduced to the main logic of citations—referring to the primary findings and claims when citing the work of other scholars.

Section 3   What's your style?

You will see that citation and referencing styles—how you actually cite—vary by discipline but that the basic reference information that is embedded in texts does not vary much.

Section 4   What am I reading?

Will introduce different reading material—empirical journal articles, literature reviews, book reviews—that is commonly found in social science journals. We will look at the citable points that come from findings in empirical journal articles and at claims in theoretical papers—the citational authority!

Section 5   How many do I cite?

You will learn that the number of sources you cite in essays is shaped by the number your instructor tells you to use. In a research paper, however, you will need to read and cite at least 15—20 journal articles to be able to pose a quality research question and come up with a meaningful critique.

Section 6   Does citation size matter?

Will show you that citations vary by size (and what this means!)

Section 7   Why should I use a note management system?

Will introduce a basic note management system (e.g., Reading Code Organisation Sheet) as a way of keeping track of your citable points ensuring you cite accurately and do not mistakenly misrepresent authors' work.

Section 8   Why worry about plagiarism?

Will provide concrete steps for becoming organized so as to avoid unintentional plagiarism in your work.

What am I supposed to cite?

10 second
summary

You should cite authors' work on their main findings or claims, whether they emerge from quantitative and qualitative analysis of data or through argumentation.

How you cite is determined by the discipline-specific styles, but what you cite is the citable point from the texts that you are reading. You should cite:

- Result of Findings (ROF) in empirical journal articles and claims. This refers to findings that emerge after data analysis.

- Result of Arguments (ROA) in theoretical and conceptual papers. This refers to claims that emerge from arguments, premises and particular conclusions. These are similar to findings in that they are citable points that authors have produced through argumentation.

Citational authority

Let's say that you have read the journal articles and books that your instructors assigned as part of course reading. You noticed that citations appeared at the end of sentences as well as the beginning of sentences, next to names in particular. At some point, you must have asked yourself, 'Just what the heck do I have to cite?' Or you may have thought to yourself, 'I understand why I have to cite, but what am I being asked to cite?' If you have asked those questions, then you are beginning to intuitively understand the idea of citational authority.

Citational authority
The findings and claims from scholarly texts that make up the primary citable points. These citable points advance the literature on a topic in substantive ways, and derive their authority from the legitimacy of their findings that contribute to the literature.

Whether the text you are reading is a book or a journal article, the principal citable point of a text is derived from the findings or a claim that are presented. It is important you understand the distinction between a finding and a claim. You need to be able to distinguish the two among the variety of texts that you are reading – from empirical journal articles to theoretical and conceptual papers.

Empirical journal articles
Published papers that derive their findings (ROF) from analysis of data. A quantitative journal article analyses large, aggregate datasets using statistical techniques while a qualitative journal article analyses analyses texts (e.g., transcripts of interviews, documents, video) using inductive methods.

A finding describes the results that are produced after the analysis of data; this data can be aggregate datasets or transcripts of interviews. However, a finding emerges after the data have been analysed in some way, using quantitative or qualitative analytical methods. Whenever you encounter a finding you should highlight it and insert the words 'ROF' next to those sentences that indicate a finding.

Result of Findings (ROF) The findings that are reported in journal articles and books that emerge from analysis of data. These findings make up the primary citable points in quantitatively and qualitatively oriented empirical papers

You will encounter findings in empirical journal articles. They will not be found in book reviews, editorials or commentaries. You will not find 'Result of Findings' (ROF) in theoretical papers or literature reviews. You will primarily find ROFs in journal articles and books that have collected data and analysed them in some principled way. Those ROFs that you have highlighted and coded as 'ROF' at the margins make up citable points. The citational authority of the texts you read comes from those findings or ROFs.

Critical literature reviews Published papers that summarize and point out the shortcomings that exist in the current state of the literature. It is a type of conceptual article as no data analysis occurs, but it may contain claims.

A claim does not emerge from analysis of data; rather it emerges from argumentation, from a set of premises to a deduction that leads to a particular conclusion. These conclusions are similar to findings in that they are the citable points. You will find these claims and arguments in conceptual and theoretical papers as well as critical literature reviews; they should be coded as 'ROA' or 'Result of Argument'.

I must warn you that ROAs are notoriously difficult to identify and code for beginners; you may confuse a general summary of previous literature as an ROA or you might overlook an ROA entirely if you unsure about how to read social science texts properly.

Summary of Previous Literature (SPL): a summary of the Results of Findings (ROFs) from previous studies that the author you are currently reading has produced. A summary condenses several complex ideas and reduces them into thematically organized paragraphs.

Result of Argument (ROA)/Claim A conclusion or set of propositions that emerge from argumentation that are similar to findings in that it becomes the citable points that authors have produced. Claims originate from a syllogistically deduced set of premises that lead to particular conclusions.

A student told us

'I know that I have to cite, but how do I pick the right bit to cite? Do I have to read everything?'

Avoid relying entirely on editorials, even if they are nice and short! You need to read each part of a journal article so you can differentiate not just between findings and claims, but also between a summary of previous literature and a critique of previous literature. You need to know what you are citing, and why.

Do not take shortcuts in your work. Read empirical journal articles, literature reviews, and conceptual papers. These type of papers tend to fall between 14 and 20 printed pages on average. In social sciences in particular, journal articles tend to be the main currency of scholarship: your professors' productivity and reputation are built on the quantity and quality of journal publications; graduate students read them like most people watch television; you should read journal articles as the principal diet for your scholarly writing. Students in English and history may be expected to read books, but the citational authority remains identical: finding comes from analysis of data; claim emerges through argumentation.

Critique of Previous Literature (CPL)
A criticism of previous scholarly works on some theoretical, methodological, and analytical grounds. CPLs usually follows SPLs, and serve as a rationale as to why your own proposed research paper is warranted.

Citational authority: The findings and claims from scholarly texts that make up the primary citable points. These citable points advance the literature on a topic in substantive ways, and derive their authority from the legitimacy of their findings that contribute to the literature.

Result of Argument (ROA)/Claim: A conclusion or set of propositions that emerge from argumentation that are similar to findings in that it becomes the citable points that authors have produced. Claims originate from a syllogistically deduced set of premises that lead to particular conclusions.

Result of Findings (ROF) The findings that are reported in journal articles and books that emerge from analysis of data. These findings make up the primary citable points in quantitatively and qualitatively oriented empirical papers.

CHECK POINT Do the typical readings in your area of study contain ROFs or ROAs?

....

....

....

....

....

....

....

'Do not take shortcuts by reading the journal article with the least number of pages. It may take twice as long to find the author's argument.'

ACTIVITY How to choose a source to cite

Ask yourself when choosing a source to cite:

☐   Does the article contain data and analysis?

☐   Am I reading an empirical journal article?

☐   Is this an editorial? Is it an argument or just a summary?

☐   Am I reading a theoretical/conceptual journal article?

☐   Is the literature review I am reading recent? If it is more than ten years old I may want to look elsewhere.

What's your style?

10 second
summary

A good citation means that you
follow the citation conventions and
referencing styles of your discipline;
there are different approaches, and
your subject or university will determine
how you cite your sources.

Citations and referencing styles vary in small details, but not in substance. Whether you are citing a book, a journal article, a government report, a newspaper article, or media content the core information remains consistent. This includes the author, publication type, title and year of publication, publisher, and page numbers; they remain identical but they vary in how they are presented stylistically. Don't feel overwhelmed about citing your sources – once you understand the logic behind the practice of citations and referencing it will make sense! Using journal articles as a primary source, I will show you the similarities and differences in major citation and referencing styles.

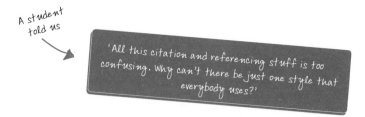

The basic ingredients in a reference

Your field of study generally determines how you cite your sources in the text itself and in the reference and the bibliography section:

- Most social science students follow the conventions of the American Psychological Association (APA), Harvard style, or the Modern Humanities Research Association's (MHRA) referencing style.

- Students who study English, literature, or history use Chicago or Modern Language Association's (MLA) referencing style.

- If you are in medical school, biomedical sciences, general science, or health-related fields of study, you are likely to use a referencing system referred to simply as the Vancouver style.

- Law students and legal studies students write and cite their sources in a way that is recognizably different from students in the social sciences. Legal writing follows the conventions of the Oxford University Standard for the Citation of Legal Authorities (OSCOLA).

Consider how a typical journal article – one of the most commonly read, cited, and referenced source of scholarship in academia – is referenced differently according to disciplinary-specific conventions. Here is the basic information related to the following journal article:

Authors:	Frank DiCataldo, Meghan Everett
Title of journal article:	Distinguishing juvenile homicide from violent juvenile offending
Journal title:	International Journal of Offender Therapy and Comparative Criminology
Year published:	2008
Volume:	52
Issue:	2
Page numbers:	158–174.

APA

DiCataldo, F., & Everett, M. (2008). Distinguishing juvenile homicide from violent juvenile offending. *International Journal of Offender Therapy and Comparative Criminology* 52(2), 158–174.

Harvard

DiCataldo, F. and Everett, M. (2008). 'Distinguishing juvenile homicide from violent juvenile offending'. *International Journal of Offender Therapy and Comparative Criminology* 52(2), pp. 158–174.

Chicago

Frank DiCataldo and Meghan Everett, "Distinguishing Juvenile Homicide From Violent Juvenile Offending," International Journal of Offender Therapy and Comparative Criminology 52, no.2 (2008): 158–174.

MLA

DiCataldo, Frank and Everett, Meghan. "Distinguishing Juvenile Homicide From Violent Juvenile Offending." International Journal of Offender Therapy and Comparative Criminology 52, no.2 (2008): 158–174. Print.

OSCOLA

F DiCataldo and M Everett, 'Distinguishing Juvenile Homicide From Violent Juvenile Offending' Intl J Off Th and Comp Crim [2008], 52 (2) IJOTC 158.

Vancouver

DiCataldo F, Everett, M. Distinguishing juvenile homicide from violent juvenile offending. Intl J of Off Th and Comp Crim. 2008; 52(2): 158-174.

You will notice that the basic information across different systems looks remarkably similar; they only differ in small stylistic conventions. Notice that styles differ as to whether first names of authors are spelled out completely in the reference or contain just the first initials. You can see that when there are multiple authors of a paper, there are differences in how they are connected to one another (e.g., 'and', '&', comma). Another difference consists in whether each word within the title of the paper is capitalized or not, as well as how the title is delineated from the rest of the information using single or double quotation marks or no quotation marks at all.

Legal and medical referencing systems use abbreviations of journal titles while social science and humanities referencing styles generally do not. You can see that most referencing styles include page numbers from start to finish, while legal referencing styles include only the first page.

These minute differences constitute the style and convention of each discipline's referencing and citation systems.

If you cited DiCataldo and Everett's[1] (2008) article within the body of your paper, then you would have included the journal article in your reference page; even if you read their paper[2] but did not cite it, but obtained relevant ideas from their work (DiCataldo & Everett, 2008), you would have to include it in a bibliography page. In-text citations describe the way authors are incorporated into the body of text (as in this paragraph) or included as footnotes or endnotes.

Understanding the conventions of your discipline and field of study is the first step towards figuring out what your course instructors will require from you in your writing assignments. As you can see, the difference in style is cosmetic, not substantial. Referencing and citations are just a matter of organising the essential pieces of information that are contained in a journal article, a book, conference proceeding, or a government report according to one's disciplinary conventions.

---

[1] DiCataldo, Frank and Everett, Meghan. "Distinguishing Juvenile Homicide From Violent Juvenile Offending." International Journal of Offender Therapy and Comparative Criminology 52, no.2 (2008): 158–174. Print.

[2] DiCataldo F, Everett, M. Distinguishing juvenile homicide from violent juvenile offending. Intl J of Off Th and Comp Crim. 2008; 52(2): 158–174.

ACTIVITY Reference styles

Here are the major citation and reference styles – what's the style used in your field? Circle it!

APA   MLA

Harvard   OSCOLA

Chicago   Vancouver

'Consider the basic information in a reference as a cake and different citation and reference style as icing and decoration.'

Once you understand the logic behind the citations and referencing systems, you should be able to understand their cosmetic character. You just have to find your style and stick to it!

What am I reading?

10 second
summary

The sources that you cite to support
your essay or paper should come
from the findings and claims that
are contained in the empirical and
conceptual texts you are reading.

What you cite is not just shaped by the citation conventions and styles of your discipline (how you cite) but by the type of scholarly text that you are reading. If your discipline's norms dictate that you read books (e.g., history), then you should read and cite books. If journal articles are the primary scholarly texts consumed in your discipline (e.g., psychology), then read and cite journal articles.

Types of scholarly text

It is very important that you are aware of the type of academic texts that you are reading for your essays and research papers. You need to be reading scholarly sources as a way of supporting your argument or for formulating a critique of the literature.

You may find lively debates between renowned scholars who are engaged in a heated debate about a topic related to their areas of expertise. Some journals even publish editorials – personal opinions based on experience and knowledge. Even though they appear within the pages of a peer-reviewed journal, these should be avoided as a source; they make bad background reading and citing them doesn't provide support and substantiation for your work.

Research paper A writing assignment where the student must pose the research question to be answered in the paper. A research question arises after you have read sufficiently and generated a POC of your own. Although they can be lengthier, most research papers fall between 3,000 and 5,000 words or about 10 to 16 double-spaced pages.

A student told us

'How am I supposed to know what I am reading? There's lots of different stuff that I have to read for my class. How do I know what to focus on?'

CHECK POINT You should be reading

1 Empirical journal articles

2 Conceptual and theoretical journal articles

3 Critical literature reviews.

These are important sources to read as background material, and ought to be the central components in your reading list, as well in your reference section and bibliography. They are crucial because they contain key bits of information related to the topic that you have selected for your essay or research paper; they are not opinions; they are not editorials. They tend to be substantive papers that advance the literature in their disciplines. They are the basis of the literature that you will summarize and critique as a way of justifying your own paper or citations that support your own claim.

The most reliable information you should cite comes from empirical journal articles. These articles are written after the authors have collected and analysed data of some kind. The data can be surveys, numerical records, transcripts of interviews, or just documents, but what makes empirical journal articles such important sources in academic writing is that they have passed the rigours of the peer review process.

Peer reviewed articles – material that has been reviewed, checked and approved by other experts in the field, usually other academics.

e.g., Kim, E. H., Hogge, I., Ji, P., Shim, Y.R., & Lothspeich, C. (2014). Hwa-Byung among middle-aged Korean women: Family relationships, gender-role attitudes, and self-esteem. *Health Care for Women International*, 35, 495–511.

Whether the analysis is quantitative (i.e., statistical) or qualitative (i.e., inductive), the paper's primary findings emerge from the analysis of data. This collection of data, followed by analysis, and write-up of the results is the golden standard of social scientific writing.

There are journal articles that are based not on analysis of data, but on a critical reinterpretation of the existing literature. Most law review articles, integrative reviews, critical literature reviews, and theoretical and conceptual papers tend to be of this variety:

e.g., Rawls, J. (1951). Outline of a decision procedure for ethics. *Philosophical Review*, 60(2), 177–197.

This type of paper tends to have dense prose of summaries and critiques, but you can come out on top if you remember that a claim is the citable point! Theoretical papers tend to be lengthy, so they are not easy to read; but if you keep asking yourself, 'what is the author's main point?' then those reminders will help you keep on track. When you come across what looks like an important claim, you should highlight and make a note of them. These steps will help prevent you from becoming lost.

There are some simple things you can do to adopt a scholarly attitude during your undergraduate years:

- It is especially important to read and understand as much as you can, you are building the foundational knowledge in your discipline

- Don't just read the introduction and the conclusion. You should read everything, especially the literature review and the methods section

- Try to read more than one article on each topic. You need to understand how the topic has evolved over time; you need to 'see' the recurring trends, patterns and themes in the literature.

If you take shortcuts, you will not learn the difference between a summary and a finding. A summary is a recurring pattern and theme in the literature. If you cite a summary as a finding, and continue citing this way, then you will be attributing statements to the author that they did not intend. This practice is the essence of plagiarism and academic misconduct.

Scholarly texts you should cite in your papers – which ones have you read?

☐ Empirical journal articles

☐ Theoretical/conceptual journal articles

☐ Critical literature reviews

☐ Books

☐ Government reports

Choosing journals

Can you identify the top five journals in your area of study?

1 ....

2 ....

3 ....

4 ....

5 ....

It is important to read high-quality sources, such as empirical journal articles. When you read reputable sources, you can then go on to cite the reputable sources. Selecting the right readings is no small task; it constitutes one of the fundamental steps in the pre-writing process.

'Taking shortcuts in your work is the fastest route to committing plagiarism.'

Identifying types of references

Match the references on the left with the corresponding type of text on the right by drawing an arrow.

Santtila, P., Laukkanen, M., & Zappala, A. (2007). Crime behaviors and distance travelled in homicides and rapes. *Journal of Investigative Psychology and Offender Profiling, 4, 1–15.*

Book review

Kim, J.M. (2015). Review of Wrongful Deaths: Selected Inquest Records from Nineteenth-Century Korea. Compiled and translated by Sun Joo Kim and Jung Won Kim. Seattle: University of Washington Press, 2014. xv, 253 pp. $75.00 (cloth); $25.58 (paper). *The Journal of Asian Studies*, 74, 1, 228–230.

Critical literature review

Gershenfeld, S. (2014). A review of undergraduate mentoring programs. *Review of Educational Research*, 84,3, 365–391.

Empirical journal article

Cope, K.C. (2010). The age of discipline: the relevance of age to the reasonableness of corporal punishment. *Law and Contemporary Problems*, 73, 167–188.

Theoretical journal article

Congratulations

You have learned why you have to cite and what you are supposed to cite. You know the citation style you should use and how this fits with the material you are reading.

Now we turn to the specifics of how many sources you should cite. We look at the tools that will help you cite the right stuff with confidence – and avoid plagiarism.

How many do I cite?

10 second
summary

The number depends on the type
of paper or essay that your course
instructor has assigned. Research
papers generally require more citations
and references than essays.

The number of sources you should cite depends on the type of writing assignment that you have been given. If your course instructor has asked you to read and incorporate eight journal articles as sources, you should read the assigned number. If your instructor has assigned a research paper without stating how many sources you should use, then you should read until you begin to 'see' the work that is missing in the current literature. Identifying these gaps will help you to create a research question, which you will then answer in your paper.

Source requirements

Almost every student who has been assigned an essay or a research paper has asked 'how many do I cite?' at some point. The answer hinges on another question that has to be answered first: **what type of a writing project have you been assigned?**

If your instructor has already given you the question to answer in your essay, the number of sources that you should cite is probably embedded in the assignment. For example:

- discuss how nutrition affects academic performance (incorporate five to seven scholarly sources to support your argument). Also, what your instructors wants you to do in the essay is already present in the question (e.g., discuss, analyse, compare, contrast, reconcile).

- most 1,000 to 2,000 word essays require around five to eight sources. Your instructor expects you to support your argument and claim by incorporating the specified number of scholarly sources (i.e., peer-reviewed journal articles, books, government reports).

If your writing assignment entails a full-blown research paper where you are expected to read through the literature on a topic of your selection, followed by the posing and answering of a research question then the answer to 'how many' becomes a bit more complicated. It is a variation of another question: **how much do I have to read in order to write my paper?**

Writing your own research paper requires that you thoroughly understand the literature on the topic that you have selected. If you need to ask a research question there are two central components:

1   Have you read enough about a topic so that you are able to 'see' the recurring themes in the literature?

2   Have you read enough so that you are beginning to 'see' the work
    that has not been done in the literature?

Recognizing that a gap exists in the literature will enable you to formulate
a research question. A gap in research is a shortcoming; it means that
the current state of the knowledge is incomplete – missing something.
You ask a research question because others have not asked it before or
because the answers that were provided missed the mark in some way.
You ask a research question as a way of addressing this gap that exists
in the literature.

Most papers assigned at university tend to be essays; these set the
scope of your answer by limiting its scope. Essays control how much
you can write, how many sources you can cite, and how you should
answer the question. Answers to essays tend to be structured by the
verbs that are posed in the question (e.g., analyse, discuss, compare,
contrast).

If you have write a research paper where you have to comb through the
literature, find a shortcoming, and remedy it somehow, then the minimum
number of sources you should cite falls somewhere between 15 and 20.
Reading through 15 up-to-date peer reviewed journal articles will allow
you to 'see' the recurring themes in the literature.

You need to read enough to arrive at a
Point of Critique (POC). This refers to the
grounds on which a reading can be cri-
tiqued; once you have judged the literature you form a criticism of it, which then
leads to a research question. This usually
emerges between reading through 20 and
25 journal articles.

Point of Critique (POC):
A deficiency in the current
article or literature that
'appears' after reading
sufficiently on a given
topic. A POC logically
leads to a CPL which you
(the student) could use as
a way of advancing the
literature by remedying
the gap that exists for a
paper.

You have to read the right stuff. Understanding the broader theme and the shortcomings in the literature emerges only after you have read relevant and up-to-date research in your discipline. That criterion is met with peer-reviewed, empirical journal articles and critical literature reviews that are published in journals.

- If your instructor assigns an essay, the number of sources that you have to use and cite will tend to be included in the assignment itself. This figure typically falls around five to eight sources.

- If your instructor has assigned you a research paper, you will have to read at least 15 journal articles to generate a research question of your own.

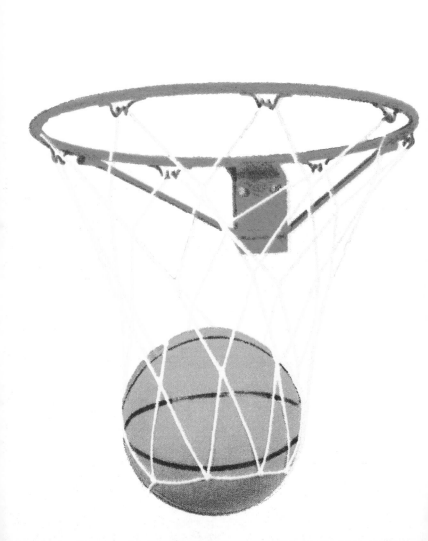

# What to write

Which of the below are you writing today?

☐ **Point of Critique (POC)**: a deficiency in the current article or literature that 'appears' after reading sufficiently on a topic. A POC logically leads to a Critique of Previous Literature (CPL) which you could use as a way of advancing the literature by remedying the gap that exists for a paper.

☐ **Essay**: the most common type of writing assignment where the instructor poses the question to be answered in the essay. Essays tend to fall between 1,000 and 2,000 words or about 4 to 8 double-spaced pages.

☐ **Research paper**: A writing assignment where the student must pose the research question to be answered in the paper. A research question comes after you have read sufficiently and generate a POC of your own. Although they can be lengthier, most research papers fall between 3,000 and 5,000 words or about 10 to 16 double-spaced pages.

A student told us

'Why do I have to read so much? No one ever told me that I have to read that much for a research paper! Research is a lot of work!'

It is easy to underestimate the amount of work that is involved in research. Research is strenuous work. Just being able to ask a research question takes a tremendous amount of preparation. However, asking the right research question is just the beginning.

'Research entails seeing an absence—
what is not there.'

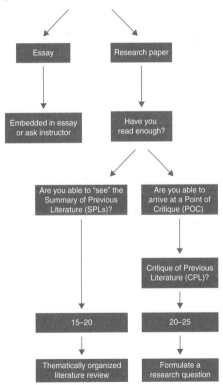

How many sources do I use?

What type of a writing project have I been assigned?

| Essay | Research paper |

Essay → Embedded in essay or ask instructor

Research paper → Have you read enough?

Are you able to "see" the Summary of Previous Literature (SPLs)?

Are you able to arrive at a Point of Critique (POC)

Critique of Previous Literature (CPL)?

15–20

20–25

Thematically organized literature review

Formulate a research question

Does citation size matter?

10 second
summary

Citation sizes vary according to the scope of the findings and claims that are being cited. Citations come in all sizes, but medium ones tend to be most common.

Similar to fries and shakes, citations come in three different sizes: big, medium, and small.

The citations you incorporate into your essays and papers should take into consideration the function of the citation as well as its size. Big citations tend to relate to scope, depth, extent, history and coverage of a topic. Medium citations tend to relate to the generalized findings related to a topic. Small citations tend to relate to some microscopic aspect of findings related to a topic.

Citation size

The size of your citation does matter and is related to what you are citing in the first place. Remember, the primary citational authority comes from the Result of Findings (ROF) in empirical journal articles or Result of Arguments (ROAs) in theoretical/conceptual journal articles. These ROFs and ROAs convey generalized findings to readers. If I were to ask you to tell me the main findings from an empirical journal article, the answer you would provide would almost definitely lead to medium-level citations. These findings would lend authority to your citations.

If you are citing numbers, figures and statistics to illustrate a point or support your argument, then that would be an example of a small citation. For example, if you state that X percent of A [subjects] engage in Z [activity related to the topic of your paper] by citing the work of T [author], then you are using numbers to support a very particular and precise point. This type of

Theoretical/conceptual articles: published papers that use existing knowledge to synthesize and integrate a new claim (ROA). A claim emerges through syllogistic methods of argumentation rather than analysis of empirical data.

small citation is noticeably different from the general findings contained in medium-level citations. If, on the other hand, you cite previous studies and authors on the extent of the topic being covered and its history then you are engaging in a 'big' citation.

ACTIVITY Citation size

Consider the following hypothetical sentences:

'Big' citation:

The adverse impact of marijuana usage has been examined by a number of scholars across the discipline, from sociology and health sciences to criminology and education.

'Medium' citation:

Marijuana usage occurs in a social setting where definitions favourable to its use exist.

'Small' citation:

Scholars report that 55 percent of first-year university students have tried marijuana.

Do you see the difference between the big, medium, and small citations?

Big citations: citations that illustrate the scope, depth, extent, history, and relevance of a topic. They tend to be found in literature review sections or introductions, usually in the first few paragraphs of the respective sections.

Example:

The impact of marijuana usage has been examined by a number of scholars across disciplines, from sociology (CITE), health sciences (CITE), criminology (CITE) to education (CITE).

Or

The impact of marijuana usage has been examined by a number of scholars across disciplines (CITE).

Big citations tell the reader that you have read through a topic and that you can synthesize the literature. You should cite multiple studies and authors who have previously examined a topic. However, you do not need to cite every single study; select 3 to 5 key studies that illustrate the extent of coverage related to your topic.

You should be able to cite sources produced by authors in different disciplines.

You should be able to cite 3 to 5 key studies from various disciplines that have examined the adverse impact of marijuana usage.

You might be tempted to cite more in order to demonstrate your breadth, but three to five is usually enough.

You should cite one or two authors whose main finding is related to marijuana usage being related to social approval.

The citation authority comes from ROFs related to this primary finding.

Medium citations: citations that illustrate the primary findings (ROFs) from your readings. They constitute the answer that you might provide if you were asked to state the main findings or points from a journal article or a book.

Example:

Marijuana usage occurs in a social context where definitions favourable to its use exist (CITE).

'Medium' citation refers to a generalized set of findings related to marijuana usage—the factors that will facilitate its usage. It is not related to extent, scope, or other big trends. If your instructor asks you to state the main findings from a journal article or a book, your answer would warrant a medium-level citation. In this example, you would find one or two authors whose main findings are related to the occurrence of marijuana usage in socially approved contexts.

Small citations: citations that illustrate some microscopic aspect of findings from your readings. Small citations tend to refer to precise findings reported by specific studies that usually involve numerical figures and statistics.

Example:

Scholars report that 39.6 percent of first-year university students have tried marijuana (CITE).

You should be able to cite the study where you are getting this figure.

Small citations tend to be very specific and particular. They are not related to trends and patterns or generalized findings. They refer to microscopic findings reported by specific studies and authors. When you are writing essays and papers and you need support, this type of precise citation provides numeric support for the arguments and claims you are making in your texts.

Try the following exercise. Match the texts on the left with the corresponding citation size by drawing an arrow.

Primary school students whose parents have graduate degrees outperform students whose parents only finished secondary school on standardized reading tests.

small citation

The reading scores of primary school students on standardized tests have far-reaching consequences, for they have been used by educational administrators, criminal justice policy makers, politicians and correctional agency administrators as predictors for modelling growth as well as programmatic and spatial needs of their respective institutions.

medium citation

Research has found that 7.9 percent of primary school students from rural areas have to repeat reading classes.

big citation

Try the following exercise. Pick a journal article that you have been assigned to read for a class or for your essay. After you have thoroughly read through the article, identify an ROF or an ROA. Now, try to paraphrase the findings in your own words according to the size of the citation that you will need for your essay or paper.

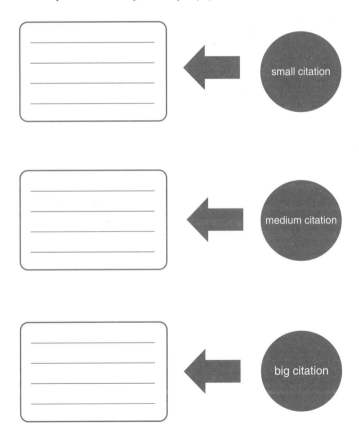

Why should I use a note management system?

10 second summary

You should use a note management system because it will save you a lot of time by organizing the ROFs from your readings into an easily retrievable format.

By using a centralized repository of your notes, you avoid the problem of flipping back to the journal articles to look up the author, year of publication, and the principal citable points. Don't risk losing citable points from your reading – keep your notes together in one spot. Organizing all the citable points in a visual format makes it easy to find what you need. Also, clearly separating ROFs from summaries enables you to avoid further confusion as to what to cite.

Reading Code Organisation Sheet (RCOS)

Using a note management system is a basic way of organizing the findings from your readings so that you do not have to go back and reread something in order to figure out the citable information.

How many times have you read something and then experienced difficulty recalling what the article was about, much less trying to discern the citable points from that article? Unless you have a photographic memory, this problem is a common one for almost everyone in academia. This problem of memory and recall is compounded as the number of sources you are expected to use increases.

Reading Code Organization Sheet (RCOS): One of several visual note management systems that uses reading codes to organize the contents of scholarly texts into an easily retrievable format

If you write an essay based on reading five peer-reviewed journal articles, keeping track of the main claims and findings may not be too difficult. If you have to recall the findings of 30 or 300 journal articles, then trying to recall the details of each article becomes a difficult task!

Writing an essay or a research paper in the social sciences is different from writing a novel. You should never begin your writing process with an empty screen. Your writing process should always begin with a note management system full of sources and an outline that provides a structure to what you want to accomplish in your paper.

Don't complete your reference list or a bibliography after you have written the main text of your paper, finish your reference list first along with your note management system and use it to organize your thoughts.

You don't want to have to refer back to the original journal articles to look up the author, year of publication, and the principal citable points. You should have that information in a centralized repository. You also need to track the recurring patterns in the literature in one place so that you do not waste time thumbing through page after page of things you have already read.

Reading Code Organisation Sheet (RCOS, pronounced R-kos): One of several visual note management systems that uses reading codes to organize the contents of scholarly texts into an easily retrievable format:

Name, year	ROF – Results of Findings	SPL – Summary of Previous Literature
8) Kim, J.M. (2015) "women's legal voice"	N=151 legal petitions 1. Korean Choson women shared similarities to Islamic women: men and women could do it equally 2. Chinese women needed a male relative 3. petitions were submitted in classical Chinese and vernacular Korean (diglossic culture in literary space)	1. petition drum installed (1401) for citizens to redress their grievances 2. sons and daughters received equal inheritances in Koroyo 3. uxorical marriage (men came to women's homes)

Name, year	ROF – Results of Findings	SPL – Summary of Previous Literature
	4. as early as 1509, women used vernacular Korean to communicate with authorities; Korean was accepted at county and provincial levels 5. gravesite dispute was one of the most commonly filed petitions in 18th and 19th centuries (removing an already existing burial and burying one's own relative in place) 6. there was no clear policy on use of mountain sides for burial purposes 7. gravestone sites became private property after 3 to 4 generations	4. women divorced 5. daughters succeeded family line 6. ancestral rites introduced

For those of you who are just beginning your university careers, you will have to read texts related to topics that you do not know much about. You will be expected to write essays and papers related to those topics that you are not familiar with. The example noted above represents a simple note taking system that I use, as well as the one I teach to my own students. Let me explain how this note taking system works.

1 Notice that this entry is the 8th journal article (authored by J.M. Kim, 2015) that I read and entered into my note management system. This journal article on women's history in premodern Korea is something that I knew little about. However, I needed to read this article as part of my literature review on women and crime.

2   There are seven ROFs that I highlighted while I was reading this journal article—these seven ROFs are the citable points. I would cite this paper if I wanted to point out that gravesite disputes were notable sources of legal conflict in premodern Korea; that gravestones eventually became private property after a few generations, despite the absence of clear governmental regulations and that women exercised agency in this regime as they could file legal petitions on their own, without the support of a male relative.

3   It would be wrong for me cite J.M. Kim on the SPL. Those themes—installation of petition drums, equal inheritances, uxorical marriages, female succession line, and ancestral rites make up the literature that J.M. Kim reviewed in her paper. These are not Kim's findings and results. Kim is merely summarizing the work that other historians have already done. Therefore, they are not citable.

As you can see, it is tough to tell the difference between a summary (SPL) and a finding (ROF). Treating a summary as a finding leads to attribution errors. That is why it is important to meticulously keep track of the citable points (ROFs). You might misattribute the findings and claims of authors if you do not separate the findings from summaries. This misattribution is the first step toward committing unintentional plagiarism. That is why you should organize your readings and the findings you encounter into a systematic note management system.

This tool will ultimately make your writing tasks easier because you will not have to struggle to find information.

Pick three journal articles that you have read. Fill in the first column with the name and year of the article that you have read. In the ROF column, fill in the main findings of the articles you have read. In the SPL column, fill in any recurring themes you see in the literature review sections of the journal articles you have read.

How many citable points does each journal article contain?

Name, year	ROF	SPL

A student told us...

'I couldn't understand why my professor was making us do RCOS. It was difficult and time consuming. But after I was done, doing RCOS gave me confidence.'

I know it can be a struggle to write research papers, particularly on subjects or topics that are new to you. It is difficult to feel confident about what you are writing. Confidence emerges once you are able to 'see' the recurring themes in the literature and as you are able to 'see' the work that has not been done in an area.

Why worry about plagiarism?

10 second
summary

You should be concerned about plagiarism since there are penalties that follow from violating university policy on academic integrity. These range from receiving a zero to suspension.

60 second summary

You want to avoid bad habits that lead to plagiarism – one of the biggest being procrastination. You should always read authors thoroughly before citing them. You should always carefully differentiate between a summary and a finding. Rather than listing passages that 'look good', you must carefully read through scholarly texts and paraphrase their ideas while fully acknowledging the source of your ideas.

Plagiarism, whether you mean to or not, is cheating. There can be serious consequences. To avoid charges of plagiarism, be sincere and approach your task with diligence and organisation.

To be clear the following practices all count as plagiarism:

- Failure to acknowledge the ideas you have gathered from someone

- Misrepresenting the work of other scholars as your own

- Citing works you have not read

- Leaving out quotation marks from a source that you have used during the course of paraphrasing

- Lifting passages just because they 'look good'

Remember – what you cite is shaped by the texts that you read; you should read reputable sources – peer-reviewed journal articles – rather than the articles with the fewest pages. You have to cite the right information – findings and claims – rather than summaries of previous literature. If you misattribute a source to an author who has made no such claims, then you have misrepresented the work of the author: plagiarism.

Here are some positive steps you can take to avoid unintentional plagiarism:

☐ Create a reading list

☐ Turn your reading list into a reference list in discipline-specific form

☐ Read, read, read

☐ Highlight and code the Result of Findings (ROFs)

☐ Organize ROFs in a note management system

☐ Create an outline of your paper

Avoid mistakes

Begin your writing project with a reading list, which then turns into a reference list. Organize the readings that you will have to complete in discipline-specific formats before you read them. Then as you read your sources, code and highlight the most consequential items that form the basis of citational authority – the ROFs. Organize these primary citable points into a note management system by authors. Create an outline of what you want to say before you start writing.

The best way to avoid allegations of plagiarism and academic misconduct is to avoid shortcuts. Shortcuts can quickly undermine the academic rigor of your work and usually involve procrastinating. If you wait until the very last minute to start your paper, you are leaving yourself vulnerable to unintended errors: bad habits nearly always follow...

Mistakes you make when you rush, you:

- Cite authors you have not read

- Skim over a paper and 'lift' passages that 'look good' rather than reading through a text thoroughly and completely

- Structure your paper using one long quotation after another instead of spending time digesting your reading

- Forget to properly acknowledge the author in the process

There is no shortcut to mastery and competence. They entail painstaking and laborious work of reading, note-taking, and paraphrasing. A true scholar approaches essays and papers with sincerity, faithfulness and humility.

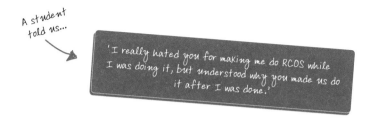

A student told us...

'I really hated you for making me do RCOS while I was doing it, but understood why you made us do it after I was done.'

You can easily avoid charges of plagiarism by using the elementary concepts related to writing: the logic and practice of citing your sources.

If you are beginning to think that all of this stuff sounds like a lot of work, you are right. But then again isn't that the whole point of a university? You attend because you want to learn—about education, literature, criminology, and sociology. Your professors expect you to demonstrate competence through written assignments in the form of essays and research papers. One way in which you become a member of the scholarly community of the university is through citing your sources. Citations are the currency with which your indebtedness to other scholars is paid. That is why it is important to cite your sources.

reading list

reference list

read and code

Reading Code Organization Sheet

outline

write

edit

'There is no shortcut to competence.'

How to know you are done

☐ Have you identified the citation and referencing style used in your field?

☐ Have you checked what is the most commonly read scholarly text in your field?

☐ Can you adjust your approach when you are writing an essay or a research paper?

☐ Do you understand where the citational authority comes from?- Are you able to identify the various citation sizes?

☐ Can you distinguish a summary (SPL) from a finding (ROF)?

☐ Can you identify the general practices that count as plagiarism?

☐ Are you familiar with the practices that count as plagiarism at your university?

☐ Have you read the relevant advice in the student handbook at your university?

Glossary

Citational authority   The findings and claims from scholarly texts that make up the primary citable points. These citable points advance the literature on a topic in substantive ways, and derive their authority from the legitimacy of their findings that contribute to the literature.

Plagiarism   a form of academic dishonesty where students fail to acknowledge the ideas gathered from a source through citation; misrepresenting the work of other scholars as one's own; citing works that have not been read; leaving out quotation marks from a source while copying exact words from a source.

Result of Findings (ROF)   The findings that are reported in journal articles and books that emerge from analysis of data. These findings make up the primary citable points in quantitatively and qualitatively oriented empirical papers.

Result of Argument (ROA)/Claim   A conclusion or set of propositions that emerge from argumentation that are similar to findings in that it becomes the citable points that authors have produced. Claims originate from a syllogistically deduced set of premises that lead to particular conclusions.

Summary of Previous Literature (SPL)   a summary of the Results of Findings (ROFs) from previous studies that the author you are currently reading has produced. A summary condenses several complex ideas into and reduces them into thematically organized paragraphs.

Critique of Previous Literature (CPL)   a criticism of previous scholarly works on some theoretical, methodological, and analytical grounds. CPLs usually follows SPLs, and serve as a rationale as to why your own proposed research paper is warranted.

Point of Critique (POC)   a deficiency in the current article or literature that 'appears' after reading sufficiently on a given topic. A POC logically leads to a CPL which you (the student) could use as a way of advancing the literature by remedying the gap that exists for a paper.

Empirical journal articles   published papers that derive their findings (ROF) from analysis of data. A quantitative journal article analyses large, aggregate datasets using statistical techniques while a qualitative journal article analyses texts (e.g., transcripts of interviews, documents, video) using inductive methods.

Theoretical/conceptual articles   published papers that use existing knowledge to synthesize and integrate a new claim (ROA). A claim emerges through syllogistic methods of argumentation rather than analysis of empirical data.

Critical literature reviews   published papers that summarize and point out the shortcomings that exist in the current state of the literature. It is a type of conceptual article as no data analysis occurs, but may contain claims.

Essay   the most common type of writing assignment where the instructor poses the question to be answered in the essay. Essays tend to fall between 1,000 and 2,000 words or about 4 to 8 double-spaced pages.

Research paper   A writing assignment where the student must pose the research question to be answered in the paper. A research question arises after you have read sufficiently and generated a POC of your own. Although they can be lengthier, most research papers fall between 3,000 and 5,000 words or about 10 to 16 double-spaced pages.

'Big' citations   citations that illustrate the scope, depth, extent, history, and relevance of a topic. They tend to be found in literature review sections or introductions, usually in the first few paragraphs of the respective sections.

'Medium' citations   citations that illustrate the primary findings (ROFs) from your readings. They constitute the answer that you might provide if you (the student) were asked to state the main findings or points from a journal article or a book.

'Small' citations   citations that illustrate some microscopic aspect of findings from your readings. Small citations tend to refer to precise findings reported by specific studies that usually involve numerical figures and statistics.

Reading Code Organisation Sheet (RCOS)   One of several visual note management systems that uses reading codes to organize the contents of scholarly texts into an easily retrievable format.

References

Kim, E. H., Hogge, I., Ji, P., Shim, Y.R., & Lothspeich, C. (2014). Hwa-Byung among middle-aged Korean women: Family relationships, gender-role attitudes, and self-esteem. *Health Care for Women International*, 35, 495–511.

Rawls, J. (1951). Outline of a decision procedure for ethics. *Philosophical Review*, 60(2), 177–197.

Walzer, M. (1988). *Spheres of Justice: A Defense of Pluralism and Equality*. New York: Basic Books.

Thomas, G. (2019). *Find Your Source*. London: SAGE.

Leicester, M., Taylor, D. (2019). *Take Great Notes*. London: SAGE.

You should cite your sources because doing so provides legitimacy and authority to your work. It demonstrates to your instructor that you have read adequately on the topic that you have selected, and that your arguments and claims have defensible support from the work of others. You have to cite your sources because good academic writing acknowledges the previous ideas of other scholars. This will become more important as you progress from writing opinion-based reflection papers to essays and research papers.

Consequences of improper citations

Let me give you some very honest answers as to why you need to cite your sources.

You need to cite reliable sources to persuade others to believe what you have to say. What qualifications, authority, and expertise do you have in order to be able to make claims of any kind? You do not. Therefore, you need to buttress your arguments and claims with scholarly support. That is what citations do: they convey to the reader—your instructor—that you have some backing in the literature, that you are not simply making stuff up. Appropriate citations also convey that you are familiar with the literature on a topic. They show that you are trying to read the work of experts and that you are well versed in what other scholars have to say.

You should also learn how to cite properly because you are literally learning a different language when you begin your studies in a university. In secondary school or two-year technical college you may have been asked to write a few (about five) paragraphs on a topic of your choosing, or you may have been asked to take a position on a social issue and then to justify and defend that position. Writing in a university is different. It requires a specific set of conventions and style for the expression of those views; you have to abide by methodological procedures and speak the language of research methodology. One way in which you demonstrate theoretical and methodological understanding is through citations.

You need to learn how to cite because university culture is very different from other institutional settings and practices. Secondary school students and international students who come to study in Western universities for the first time may not know that copying and pasting from a book or a webpage without acknowledging the authors or giving them credit is wrong. You may not think this practice is a big deal. Let me set the record straight: copying passages from another person's work and presenting them as your own, or not attributing an author's ideas and findings through citations are not acceptable practices. They are known as plagiarism and lead to charges of academic misconduct, which carry penalties.

You need to cite or else you will get in trouble. If you don't you could fail your assignment, you might fail a course altogether, you might be suspended from your university or you might be found guilty of academic misconduct. You need to accurately cite the work of authors; not doing so has big consequences. It is a core component of academic life in a university.

You should also understand that citations and their functions vary according to the type of paper that you are writing and, what you are citing. For example, in a 1,000–2,000 word essay where the question has already been posed by your instructor, you may need to cite previous works as a way of supporting a claim that you are trying to make:

Plagiarism a form of academic dishonesty where students fail to acknowledge the ideas gathered from a source through citation; misrepresenting the work of other scholars as one's own; citing works that have not been read; leaving out quotation marks from a source while copying exact words from a source.

Essay the most common type of writing assignment where the instructor poses the question to be answered in the essay. Essays tend to fall between 1,000 and 2,000 words or about 4 to 8 double-spaced pages.

ACTIVITY Discuss the impact of poor nutrition on academic performance

Let us assume that your main claim is that eating too much junk food will lead to poor academic performance. If this is the central argument you want to make in your essay, then you will probably need to find others to support your claim. Have others made a similar claim? Are there studies that show correlation between consuming junk food with low grade point averages and test scores? If so, you show support for your claim by citing the work of others.

In a research paper, citations are inserted in several places:

• After summaries to demonstrate the breadth and depth of your understanding.

• In a critique of previous literature to demonstrate that others have made similar criticisms.

• In a discussion and conclusion section showing how your ideas are similar to or different from the findings of others.

'Citations are the currency with which intellectual debts to other scholars are paid.'

Walzer, Michael, *Spheres of Justice: A Defense of Pluralism and Equality* (1988)

Policy check

Can you locate the passages that are related to plagiarism and academic misconduct in the student handbook at your university?

Why do I
have to cite?

10 second
summary

You should cite because it is a way of
acknowledging the work of others. If
you do not cite, you are committing
plagiarism.